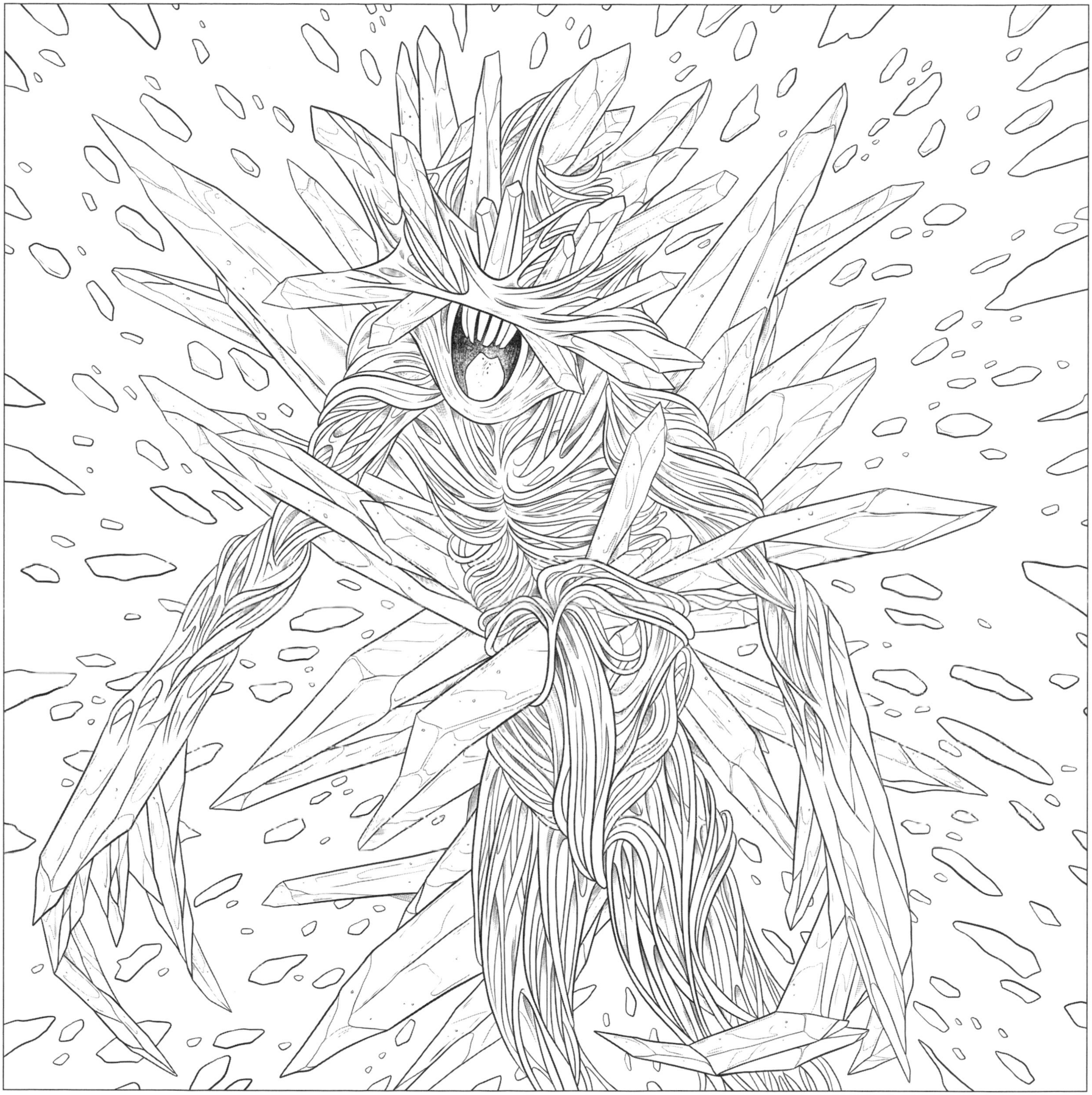

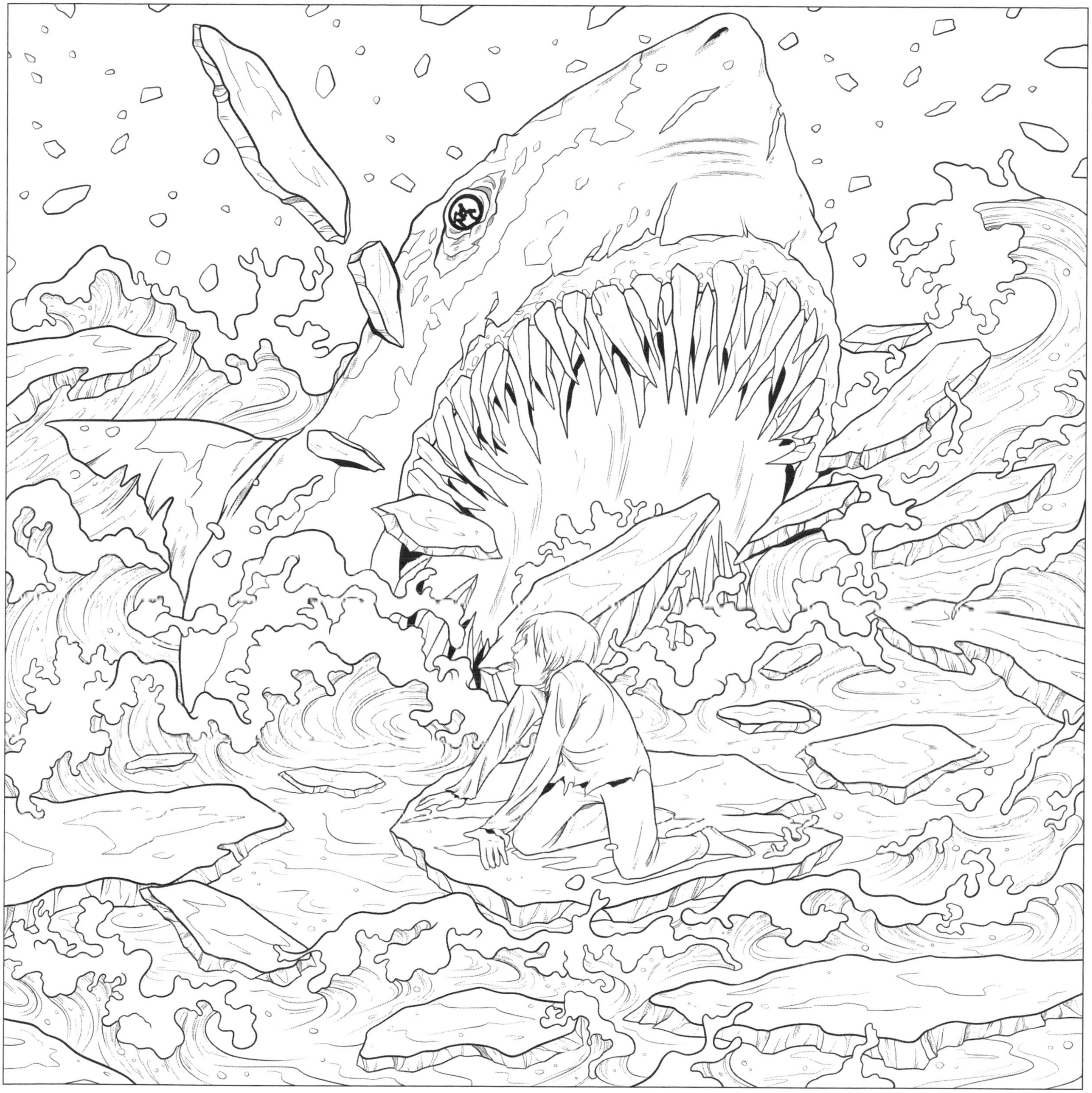

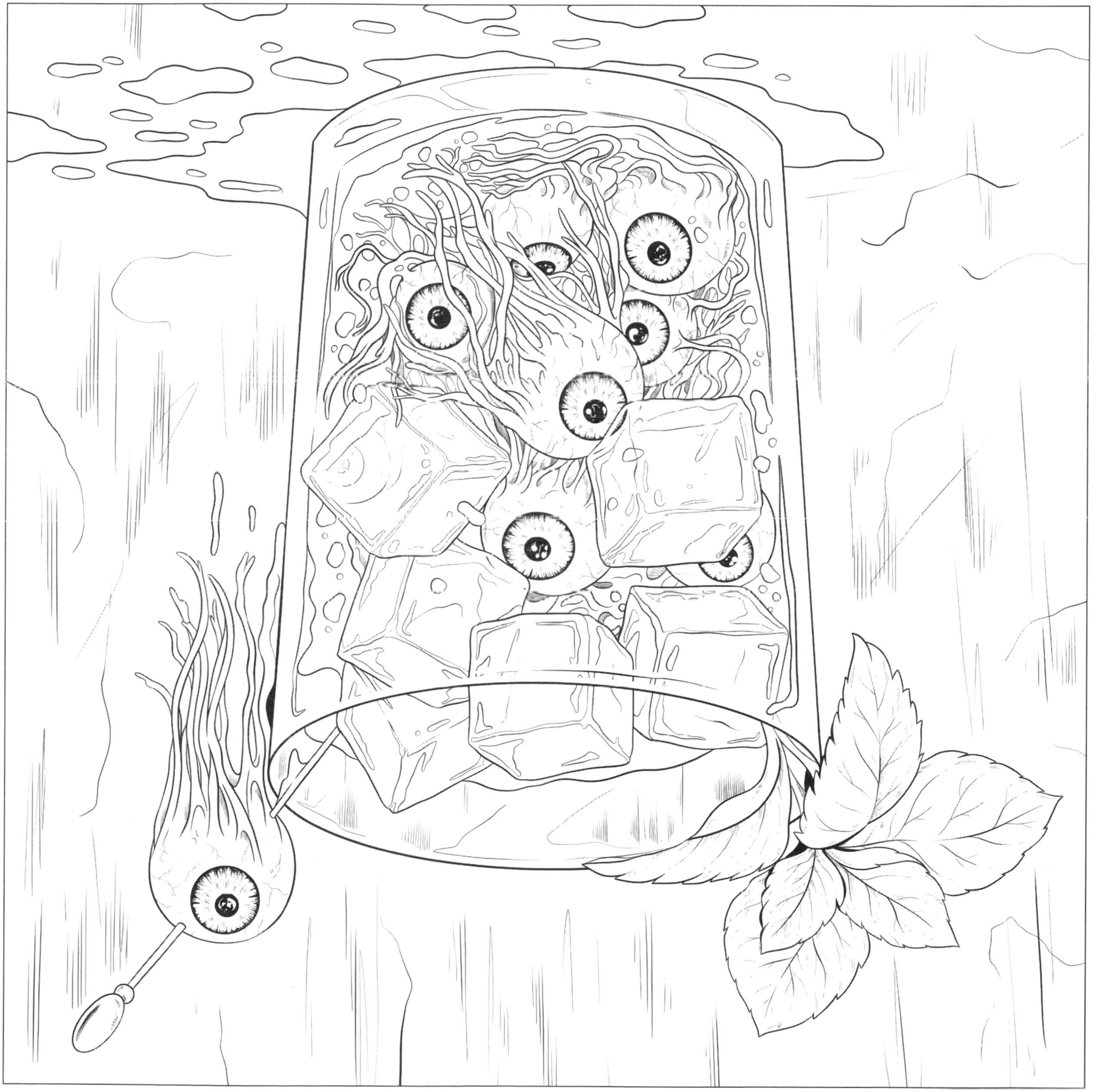

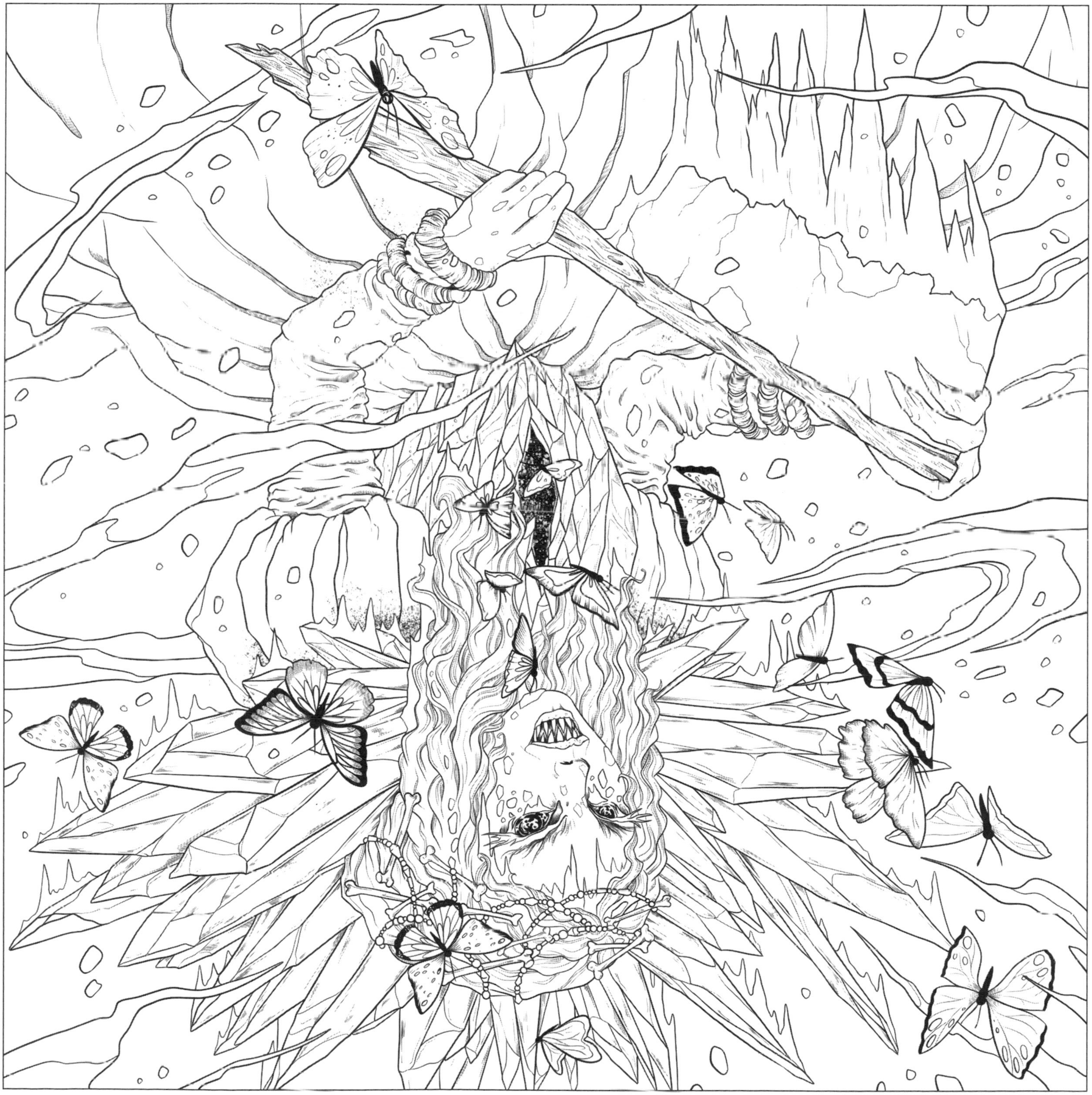

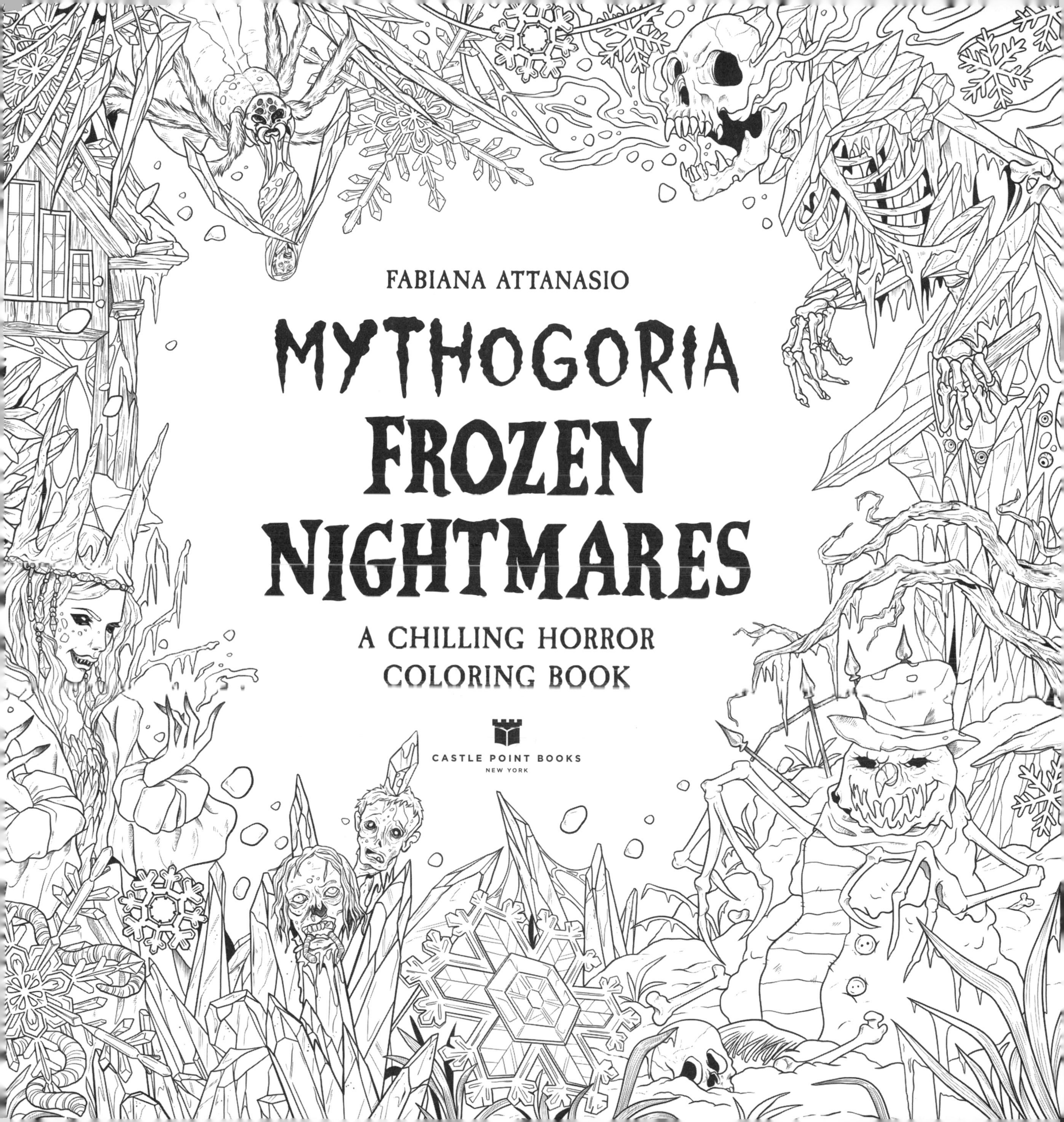

FABIANA ATTANASIO

MYTHOGORIA
FROZEN NIGHTMARES

A CHILLING HORROR COLORING BOOK

CASTLE POINT BOOKS
NEW YORK